Survival

The Ultimate Guide With 10
Outdoor Survival Tricks During
the State of Emergency
(Off the Grid Survivalist,
Prepping, Survival Stories)

By Carrie Dresden

Table of Contents

Introduction

Globally, natural disasters are frequent occurrences. Depending on the type of disaster, fatalities and damages that occur as a result are most often emotionally and financially devastating. The way to combat the effects of a natural disaster is to have a plan in place. Natural disaster preparedness can mean the difference between life and death. Being prepared for these occurrences works toward minimizing personal loss and injury as well.

There are standard plans that should be in place that applies for every disaster. These include having a communication plan, developing an emergency kit, creating checklists, and establishing escape routes. These will cover the needs for any and all natural disasters. From there, a risk assessment should be completed and based on the extreme weather that is prone to happen - which is based on the region where a person resides – specific steps should be taken to safeguard against that particular disaster.

Preparing for natural disasters is essential as with little to no warning, one may occur at any moment. Looking through history and assessing the damage and death suffered due to weather related catastrophic events, in hindsight, most affected are counting the different ways one could have been prepared to lessen the impact of the resulting tragedies. The best way to survive these events is to always be prepared.

Chapter 1: When Disaster Strikes

When a natural disaster strikes, will you be ready? As much technology and media, we currently have at our disposal, there are and have been instances where a person has a day or less than a few hours to prepare in anticipation of a natural disaster striking. Depending on the occurrence, there may be little to no warning. Yet in still, there are times when an impending catastrophe is forecasted and ultimately, it was an overestimate or an exaggeration of how damaging the effects will be.

The following question remains, how does one prepare for one of the inevitabilities of life – the wrath of "Mother Nature?" The answer is to simply to always be ready. Disaster preparedness can mean the difference between life and death in the instance of severe, life-threatening weather. If you take a poll of people who have survived disasters such as earthquakes, tornadoes or even hurricanes, undoubtedly the feedback you would receive from them is a hindsight related view. They would recall the instances where precautions or preplanning could have been taken place prior to the incident which would have resulted in weathering the disaster more effectively. Every survivor would be able to recall an instance where a certain preventative measure could have saved a life or saved a piece of meaningful property.

The old adage remains, the best cure is prevention. For disaster preparedness, the same applies – the best course of action is to have a plan in place to minimize or eliminate losses. Too many times, we live in a bubble of security, oblivious to the fact that a devastating act of nature can affect our lives at any moment. Taking a proactive instead of a reactive stance is vital in order to weather the effects of the storm – no matter which forms the storm takes.

The world we live in now is certainly not the same as the one inhabited by our parents and their parents. Different environmental factors – global warming being a significant one – has made for an environment where the weather is temperamental and unpredictable at best. A person needs to be adequately prepared for a state of emergency that is driven by the changeability of earth's elements. Always be prepared. Always have a plan.

Chapter 2: Developing a Natural Disaster Plan

Preparing Regionally

Creating an effective natural disaster plan relies on knowing the region where you are living in and the natural disasters that are more prone to occur. This acts as the cornerstone of an effective natural catastrophe plan. For the person living in California – the priority plans will primarily target earthquakes and wildfires. An individual living in New York will want to focus on hurricanes and blizzards. Ultimately, there needs to be a natural disaster plan for every kind of possible occurrence. However, the plans should be developed and prioritized according to the region and the frequency of natural disasters relative to the area.

Communication Plan

A communication plan during the time of natural disaster is vital in ensuring that everyone is accounted for and there is clarity on next steps in moving forward during such an occurrence. In the instance of a natural catastrophic event, tools of communication such as cell phones, internet or television can instantly be damaged – making communication during such an event impossible. Taking a few preemptive steps in making sure that communication is still possible even in the face of disaster increases the chances that everyone remains together – or finds their way back to one another relatively quickly– and everyone is clear on what to do next to survive.

An effective communication plan should have several parts to it. Primarily, a meeting place should be selected in the neighborhood where family members can meet up in the case of separation. Whether it is a church or school, everyone needs to be aware of where this location is and must make sure to go directly there should the situation call for it. Additionally, there needs to be a designated individual selected to be the main point of contact. Ideally, this person should be an out of state family member that, in the event of separation, family members can call to let them know they are safe. Be sure that all family members are subscribed to alerts in order to be fully aware of important communications regarding the natural disaster. Everyone should also have an in the case of emergency number (ICE) programmed into the phone as having this number will alert medical personnel on who to call in the case that someone is injured. Lastly, everyone should be familiar with how to send text messages as they are easier to send than making calls during a natural disaster occurrence. The communication plan will ensure that every member of a family stays together and can be contacted in case of separation.

Create Checklists

Creating a checklist is an important part of creating a disaster preparedness plan. A checklist ensures that a family has access to emergency contacts. The checklist also provides an overview of items that need to be completed to ensure that losses are minimized or even eliminated.

Again, since during the time of a storm there will be very little to even think, the checklist should have all important contacts such as emergency numbers – police, fire, and ambulance. The designated, out of state contact selected should also be listed under emergency numbers as well. Procedural information such as how to shut off utilities such as electricity, water, and gas or how to use emergency equipment such as a fire extinguisher should also make up the checklist. The checklist should really serve as the *how to* in navigating severe weather.

Recognize Escape Routes

The effects of a natural disaster can cause the blocking of the main entrance of the home. As such, there needs to be more than one escape route that is established and communicated to the entire family. In the instance that one escape way is blocked – there are others available that can provide an exit to safety.

Pet Care

During a disaster, one mustn't forget the pets. There needs to be a plan set in place to ensure that animals, as members of the family, are adequately covered and are taken into safety during damaging weather. A good idea would be to again, be proactive. Before a severe event (provided there is an advanced warning) arrangements should be made to place pets somewhere safe. A good idea would be to see if there are animal shelters who can hold the pet for a while or even seek the help of an out of state relative who is to watch the animal in advance of the event. If this isn't possible and there needs to be an evacuation of the home – then pets should be taken along with the family.

Chapter 3: Hurricanes

In recent years, hurricane Sandy and Katrina proved just how damaging a hurricane can be. These powerful storms have the ability to virtually cripple a person's daily life. Hurricanes are responsible for destroying homes, they have led to several deaths, and this isn't the kind of natural disaster to be taken lightly at all. Preparing for a hurricane is a must-do, as a hurricane can really develop and affect any part of the world. Failure to prepare for a hurricane is preparing to lose.

Hurricanes are season specific. Depending on the part of the world where a person resides, the probability of a hurricane occurring greatly increases. In the United States, for instance, hurricane season runs from June 1st to November 30th.

If an individual resides in a region that is prone to hurricanes – the best course of action would be to prepare before one strikes. In addition to creating a natural disaster plan as outlined in chapter 2, make an effort to protect assets by considering the purchase of flood insurance. Flood insurance protects the home and valuables in the event that a hurricane results in a deluge of water.

In the event of an impending hurricane, a person should begin the steps to prepare the home. Hurricanes are characterized by violently strong winds – in advance of one, be sure clear any loose or fallen branches. Debris should be picked up and discarded. Really any object outside the home that can be moved by the wind should be cleared. Be sure to secure any loose rain gutters and it would be a good idea purchase a generator as power if often lost in the aftermath of a hurricane. Be sure to create an emergency supply kit. This kit should contain all the essentials needed should a person be forced to evacuate. The emergency supply kit should have cash, flashlights, batteries, important documents and a can or two of non-perishable food.

Most importantly, keep apprised of the latest communications regarding the hurricane. If evacuation is ordered, be sure to grab the emergency supply kit and comply with the evacuation request. Too many people make the attempt to "ride out" the storm and end up paying for it with their lives. A home, valuables, these things are replaceable. A person's life cannot be. Be smart. If you are ordered to leave – then leave. This ensures the best possible result of surviving a hurricane.

Chapter 4: Earthquakes

Of all natural disasters, an earthquake has got to be one of the more feared of natural disasters. Typified by the sudden shaking caused by movement under the surface, the devastation that can be caused by the shaking of the ground can cause landslides or avalanches – both which can destroy homes, injure and kill people.

The most recent high-profile earthquake happened in January 2010. An earthquake with a magnitude of 7.0 struck the already ailing country of Haiti, causing the deaths of 160,000 people. In addition to the deaths, approximately 1 million people lost their homes and were displaced. Sufficed to say, earthquakes are a very serious natural disaster.

Preparing for an earthquake undoubtedly requires having a natural disaster plan in place. In addition to this, there are specific actions that can be taken to ensure the greater likelihood that lives are saved should a high magnitude earthquake occur.

Beforehand – especially if a person lives in a region prone to earthquakes – a survey should be done of the home to identify safe areas to run to in the event of an earthquake. Good areas to seek refuge would be under a very sturdy table or the interior of a wall. One should also secure items (bookcases, dressers, etc.) that can topple over during an earthquake. Additionally, a person should practice the "drop, cover, and hold on" method. This means a person immediately falls to the ground, covers their head with their arms and keep the position. This makes it so that the person is able to eventually move to safety while protecting themselves from falling debris. During the onset of an earthquake, there is limited time to think. The drop, cover, and hold exercise should be practiced until it becomes instinctual in the event of an earthquake.

Again, during an earthquake – be sure to immediately go into the drop, cover, and hold on the position. If a person finds themselves in a building and they are in danger of falling debris, they should seek to crawl and find cover under a sturdy piece of furniture, however, they should not make an attempt to exit a building. If an individual finds themselves outside during the onset of an earthquake, they should quickly move away from buildings, utility poles and street lights and drop, cover, and hold until the shaking stops.

Chapter 5: Tornadoes

A tornado is a natural disaster that includes a fiercely rotating wind tunnel that moves both at sea and on the ground. Known as the world's most violent storms, this column of wind is a destructive one with the power to uplift substantial structures such as houses or automobiles. While there are tornados that may pass through an empty field causing little to no damage, a hurricane passing through a populated city is potent enough to completely decimate an area within mere seconds. Furthermore, a tornado can gather rather quickly – not allowing for any advance warning.

If a person resides in a region that is prone to tornadoes, a good course of action would be to consider building a shelter or a safe room within the dwelling. A safe room is one that can withstand super strong winds. This is where the family should go to until the storm passes through. A basement would be the optimal area to build one of these as a basement is below ground level– however, if the home does not have a basement, then an interior room may be used instead. When building a safe room, the walls of this shelter should be separated from the walls of the home so that if the home is destroyed, the walls can still withstand the high winds. There are safe rooms that are created for the very purpose of withstanding the effects of a tornado, one might even consider purchasing one of these and having it installed. They do tend to run a little pricey, however, there is no cost as great as knowing a person's family has a safe place to go to should a tornado approach.

Tornado preparedness means always keep on top of weather updated and alerts. In addition to this, one should watch the weather, taking note of any storm like weather that seems to be approaching. If a tornado advisory does go out, shelter needs to be sought immediately. If an individual finds themselves outside, they should again, look for shelter and be sure to look out for flying debris which accounts for most of the injuries and fatalities during a tornado. A person should never try to outdrive a tornado. Surviving a potentially fatal occurrence like a tornado is much easier if a person has taken all the necessary steps to prepare.

Chapter 6: Wild Fires

A common natural disaster in regions such as California, wildfires are destructive fires that spread alarmingly quickly over woodland or brush. Wildfires are an extremely aggressive fire to fight. These type of flames are responsible for destroying several acres of beautiful woodland. Wildfires often start with no advance warning and are likely to occur during times of little rain as this makes woodlands dry and more susceptible to burning. Again, while being common in certain states, wildfires can occur almost anywhere.

Wildfires have claimed the lives of firefighters as well as destroying structures such as houses. Due to the immense heat that is given off by these fires, they are also responsible for causing the soil to melt, which ultimately leads to landslides. California's largest wildfire in the state's history struck in 2007. Known as the Cedar fire, this was a mega blaze, spanning approximately 270,000 acres. The Cedar fires also destroyed 38 homes, causing the displacement of several families. Wildfires are a natural disaster capable of much damage.

Since the home is most susceptible to damage from a wildfire, preparing for this disaster means taking the appropriate steps to prepare the home. If a person resides in an area where there is a higher likelihood of wildfires, there are specific steps that should be taken to minimize losses in the event of a wildfire. Steps should be taken to make the home resistant to catching fires. Among these, flammable materials or debris that can burn easily should be eliminated around the home. Roofs and gutters should regularly be cleaned and leaves always cleared from the ground.

When building additional areas of the home, fire resistant materials should be used for construction. It is also a good idea to create and maintain an area about 30 feet away from the home that is resistant to fire. A good idea is creating a concrete slab that is free of any debris. Additionally, a person should always be prepared – keep large containers (i.e. trash cans) of water in several spots around the property. There should always be a hose long enough to get to any area of the house.

Always keep apprised of alerts. If an evacuation is ordered, be sure to comply. Wildfires spread extremely quickly; evacuating when alerted to do so such be a split second decision of flight.

Chapter 7: Drought

Drought is a natural occurrence that comes about when the water supply in an area is extremely low. Unlike the other severe weather conditions outlined here, drought is not a natural disaster by means of impact. Instead, the dangers associated with a drought are more on a macro scale as the destruction that occurs with a drought are more of a ripple effect. Waters is needed to grow food; if food is not grown, people do not eat – famine occurs. We need water to maintain ourselves hygienically. An absence of essentials such as baths and brushing will cause a disruption in an individual's quality of life. Animals need water to survive – again, livestock, not surviving contributes to famine as well. Water powers natural resources such as electricity. A shortage of water in the form of a drought can lead to the eventual death of both humans as well as a major, large-scale disruption in a person's life.

On an individual level, a person should always be prepared in case a drought develops in an area. The main focus of preparing for this kind of occurrence lies in water conservation. During the drought is the time to restrict activities in an effort to save water. Primarily, always follow instructions from local state government regarding minimizing water use.

Additionally – take care that nothing is done in excess. For instance, for the person brushing their teeth or shaving – water should not be running while these activities are being done. Avoid flushing the toilet unnecessarily; instead of depositing toilet paper in the toilet – opt for a trash can instead. If during a drought there are plants that need to be maintained – a good tip would be to catch water used during a shower and use this to water plants. When washing dishes, be sure to use two containers – one with soapy water and another with clean water to rinse. If a person relies on a dishwashing machine, the machine should not be run until the machine is full of dishes. Lawns should not be overwatered.

Most importantly, if a person lives in an area that is known for drought, stockpiling water would be the best way to prepare. Ideally, the amount of water recommended to store is two gallons per person for each day. There should be a two weeks supply of water for each family member in preparation for a drought. Therefore, for a family of 4, 8 gallons would cover the family per day. For a two week supply, the total number of gallons that should be stored is 112. The best way to store water is in a PBA free 5-gallon water bottle. With these simple steps, a person is able to minimize the quality of life disruptions that can be caused by drought.

Chapter 8: Landslides

The Oso landslide in Washington is the deadliest landslide to ever happen in U.S history. Occurring on March 22, 2014, this landslide claimed the lives of 43 people and caused an unbelievable amount of mass destruction. Defined as a sliding down of a mass of earth or rock down a mountain or hill, these devastating occurrences most often happen in mountainous states such California, Oregon, and Washington. Landslides are an extremely serious and potentially fatal natural disaster, preparing for one of these is a must in order to minimize loss of both life and property.

An individual living in a region that is susceptible to landslides should take a careful and strategic approach to selecting where they choose to live. Becoming familiar with the area should be the first steps taken. A good way to do this would be to check local offices to see if this is an area prone to landslides. Be certain to take a survey of the area, as a person would want to avoid making a home near steep hills or close to mountain edges. A homeowner living in an area prone to landslides may want to protect their home by purchasing additional insurance that would cover damage occurring from this type of disaster. They may want to contact contractors as well to inquire about ways to incorporate reinforcing structures to the home that would make it less susceptible to damage in the event of a landslide. An example of such would be flexible pipe fittings which are better able to resist destruction.

Landslides usually occur with storms. If a severe storm is happening, the best course of action would be to stay awake and remain alert. Many fatalities occur when people are asleep during the onset of a landslide. In accordance with keeping alert, the warning signs of a landslide should be looked out for as well. These include sounds of falling debris including rocks falling and tree branches breaking. If a person finds themselves in the path of a landslide, they should quickly move away from its path. Low lying areas should be avoided. In the event, there is debris flow and an individual is not able to get out of the way, the best course of action for an individual to take would be to roll themselves into a ball, covering his or her head. Surviving landslides means being alert and being ready to move quickly.

Chapter 9: Extreme Cold & Winter Weather

The damages of extreme cold associated with winter weather are serious and may even be fatal. Again, unlike many of the conditions outlined above, extreme cold is a non-impact type of natural disaster. Fatalities from an extreme cold can stem from prolonged exposure to cold or accidents occurring from fallen trees and icy roads. Whatever the damage or kind of death likely that are due to cold, it is extremely important to take the necessary safeguards in ensuring a safe winter.

During the onset of winter, one should always be prepared for the severe decrease of temperatures as well as the storms to follow. Primarily, a person should begin this season with sufficient fuel to heat the home. In the case where leaving the home may not be a possibility due to frigid temperatures, the home needs to be adequately heated to last several days. Having a good supply of warm clothing as well as comforters is a must as well. The following supplies should always be on hand and readily available: salt to break dissolve ice that may form, sand to provide traction to vehicles in the case of a storm as well as a shovel for snow removal. Additionally, all drafts should be identified and sealed within the home.

In the period of harsh weather and storming, undoubtedly the best course of action is to stay inside. The safest place to be when there is severely cold weather is in the home. Again, be sure to conserve heating fuel. It may be a good idea to turn the heat off to certain rooms as to save on heating. A person should be dressed warmly wearing several layers of clothing in order to remain warm. If shoveling needs to be done during cold weather, an individual should be careful not to over to it by means of over exertion. Over exerting oneself during shoveling can bring about conditions such as a heart attack. Heart attacks during shoveling contribute to a significant number of fatalities during severely cold weather.

If travel is unavoidable, be sure to travel during the day, driving slowly and carefully. A good idea would be to let family or friends know that you are out and what your destination is and the expected time of arrival. In the event there is an accident, someone will be aware of travel routes, knowing where to send assistance. Again, the person traveling should dress very warmly, being careful not to expose any skin. Should a storm cause someone to become trapped in their vehicle, the person should remain in the car, putting on hazards lights until someone is able to stop by and provide assistance. The only instance when a person should leave their vehicle is when there is a visible location where shelter can be sought that is within walking distance. Conserving gas is crucial during this time.

The trapped person should be sure to run the engine and heat for ten minutes at a time to keep warm, being sure to lower the window slightly to keep from succumbing to carbon monoxide poisoning. If traveling with others in the car, passengers should get close to one another, using body heat to keep warm. Jackets should be used as blankets.

In this set of circumstances, knowing the signs of hypothermia and frostbite is absolutely necessary. Major symptoms of frostbite include the loss of feeling in parts of the body such as fingers, toes, ears, and the nose. Symptoms of hypothermia include shivering, mental disorientation, slurred speech and lethargy. Should any of these symptoms occur, medical attention is needed immediately. Surviving cold weather and extreme storms means taking precautions to remain inside during inclement weather. Should that not be possible, the best course of action would be to proceed with travel extremely cautiously.

Chapter 10: Extreme Heat

Extreme heat is no doubt a dangerous natural event for a person to find themselves in. Heat kills by means of pushing the body to its limits. With extreme heat, liquids found in the body evaporate, and when this happens, the body must work additionally hard to withstand a normal body temperature. The primary target population at risk from extreme heat and humidity are the elderly and those who are of ill health. Severe heat for this groups causes deaths stemming from heat stroke. While the elderly and sick are at highest risk from extreme heat, younger, healthier people are at risk for heated-related fatalities as well. Oblivious to the inherent dangers associated with exercising outdoors in hot weather; many are unknowingly putting themselves at risk. Like the elderly, fatalities from heat stroke are possible if anyone chooses a time of extreme heat to exercise. In addition to heat stroke, damages from over exerting oneself in extreme heat include heat cramps, fainting spells as well heat exhaustion. Heat-related deaths have claimed the lives of thousands of people, living in the United States alone. Protecting oneself from heat-related death or injury, a person should put practices into play which work towards helping to keep a normal body temperature during extremely hot weather.

First off, during a heat wave, it is advised that a person should remain indoors as much as possible. Any outdoor extracurricular activities or any plans to exercise should be suspended until the heat wave breaks. Strenuous housework should be avoided. A good proactive step would be to purchase air conditioning units before a heat wave emerges, especially if one lives in an area prone to extreme heat. In the event that air conditioning is not available, it is advised to stay on the lowest floor, with little to no exposure to sunshine. If a person does need to leave home, public buildings such as offices, shopping malls or libraries are a good choice as these structures always have central air conditioning and the circulating air found in these places is beneficial to the body.

To help maintain body temperature and help avoid heat stroke, an individual should drink plenty of water. Staying hydrated is key to keeping healthy during a heat wave. Alcoholic drinks and caffeine should be avoided.

The elderly should always be checked on, especially if there is no air conditioning where they reside and they live alone. Pets should also be monitored as well, being sure to look for signs of heat exhaustion. Children or pets should never be left in a closed vehicle during extremely hot weather as this will, without a doubt, lead to death. The key to protecting oneself from the dangers of extreme heat lie in taking the necessary steps to safeguard and maintain a normal body temperature.

Conclusion

Always be prepared. Nature is nature and as such, extreme weather conditions will always occur – this is certainly one of life's inevitabilities. Preparing for these events means understanding a person's risk and accordingly putting safeguards in place to minimize loss and avoid death.

There are certain aspects of natural disaster preparation that are standard and covers the needs of every occurrence. Among these, having a plan of communication as well as a disaster preparation kit plays a central role. Being able to communicate during a disaster and having important documents as well as essentials needed to endure a catastrophic natural event are essentials needed through any and all disasters.

Moreover, additional steps need to be taken based on region as well as risk. If the area is prone to a certain kind of weather condition, preparation targeted towards that natural disaster should be taken before hand. For instance, a person residing in an area prone to hurricane activity should take steps to safeguard against damage that can be caused by a hurricane.

The best chance a person has to survive a natural disaster is to put a plan in place and to always be prepared.

www.ingramcontent.com/pod-product-compliance
Lightning Source LLC
Chambersburg PA
CBHW072022290526
45787CB00014B/1761